To my dearest father, Rudy, who led by example
and showed us the true meaning of sacrifice
and unconditional love for family
—P.T.

To my parents, George and Leonora.
For leaving the life they knew
to create a better future for us
—D.D.

The art for this book was created digitally.

Cataloging-in-Publication Data has been applied for and may
be obtained from the Library of Congress.

ISBN 978-1-4197-5528-6

Text © 2023 Patricia Tanumihardja
Illustrations © 2023 Derek Desierto
Book design by Heather Kelly

Printed and bound in China
10 9 8 7 6 5 4 3 2 1

Abrams Books for Young Readers are available at special discounts when purchased in quantity for
premiums and promotions as well as fundraising or educational use. Special editions can also be created to specification.
For details, contact specialsales@abramsbooks.com or the address below.

Abrams® is a registered trademark of Harry N. Abrams, Inc.

ABRAMS The Art of Books
195 Broadway, New York, NY 10007
abramsbooks.com

Jimmy's Shoes

The Story of Jimmy Choo, Shoemaker to a Princess

written by
Patricia Tanumihardja

illustrated by
Derek Desierto

Abrams Books for Young Readers
New York

On the tropical island of Penang, where waves crashed onto white sandy beaches,

pretty orchids dotted verdant hills,
and hawkers crowded lively streets,

Jimmy was born into a family of shoemakers.

As a little boy, Jimmy sat at his father's knee
and watched skilled hands
cut, stitch, and shape
leather into works of art.

When he was eleven, Jimmy made his
first pair of shoes with his father's help

—a pair of leather slippers for his mother.

A year later, Jimmy became a full-time apprentice in his father's workshop.

And his education took on a different shape.

For the next few years, Jimmy worked diligently by his father's side. He learned how to make a pair of shoes from start to finish.

STEP 1: Take detailed measurements of the arch and each and every angle of the foot.

STEP 2: Create a wooden or plastic mold called a last.

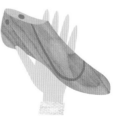

STEP 3: Trace the shoe pattern on leather or fabric.

STEP 4: Cut the pattern out to form the upper.

STEP 5: Shape the upper around the last.

STEP 6: Hand-stitch the upper to the sole.

STEP 7: Build the heel layer by layer on each shoe (for oxfords) or wrap fabric around the heel (for stilettos).

STEP 8: Attach the heel.

STEP 9: Trim the sole and remove the last.

STEP 10: Insert fine liners inside the shoe.

The more Jimmy worked in the shop, the more he loved making shoes.

Unfortunately, a turn in Penang's economy ruined Jimmy's future as a shoemaker on the island. However, his father told him that a talented shoemaker can make a good living traveling the world. And Jimmy believed him.

When Jimmy was in his late teens, he moved to London, his strong work ethic and talent in tow.

Even though Jimmy had relatives in London, adapting to his new life was challenging.

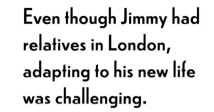

He struggled with the language, new customs, and unfamiliar foods.

To make ends meet, he swept floors, cleaned toilets, and often survived on one meal a day.

While in London, Jimmy heard about Cordwainers Technical College, a trade school that had been training shoemakers for over a century.

He enrolled, eager to supplement the skills he learned from his father.

Unlike many of his classmates, Jimmy hadn't gone to art school, and his design sketches were unpolished.

Despite many obstacles, Jimmy
was determined to succeed.
He studied shoemaking by day

and English by night,

and practiced, practiced, practiced.

Soon, Jimmy's English improved, his sketches went from rough to refined, and his design talent sparkled. All his hard work paid off, and Jimmy graduated with distinction.

Jimmy's dream was to open his own shoemaking business, just as his father had. To help him set up his new business, his mother gave him her life savings, and both parents moved to London. They believed in him and wanted him to succeed.

He couldn't let them down.

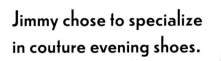

Jimmy chose to specialize in couture evening shoes.

Couture shoes are handmade exclusively for the customer using expensive, high-quality materials.

He envisioned uniquely designed shoes that fit like Cinderella's glass slippers.

Jimmy rented a tiny space in a dilapidated
redbrick building where he worked hard from
dawn till dusk, cutting, stitching, beading.
His designs were inspired by the vibrant
flowers, brilliant birds, and graceful
architecture of his homeland.

At first, Jimmy sold his shoes under the brand Lucky Shoes.

But Jimmy was not so lucky. He sold only one or two pairs a week.

Looking around the market, Jimmy noticed that people were buying shoes, just not *his* shoes. He realized he had to rethink his strategy.

Jimmy started to promote himself more and forged relationships with magazine editors and fashion designers. Now, instead of making shoes and hoping someone would buy them, Jimmy designed shoes on demand . . .

JIMMY

CHOO!

. . . for runway designers . . . for fashion shoots . . . and for clients who trickled into his workshop. Through word of mouth, his reputation for reasonably priced, one-of-a-kind shoes spread.

Jimmy's big break came when his shoes were showcased at London Fashion Week, the city's biggest fashion event.

Then, a major fashion magazine featured his shoes in an eight-page spread, boosting his business tremendously.

Celebrities placed orders. High-profile fashion designers used Jimmy's shoes in their runway shows.

There were times when Jimmy was so busy, he didn't go home for days!

Jimmy was working hard.
His shoes were getting attention,
but he was still not making much money.

One day, Jimmy got a call.
Did Jimmy want to make shoes
for a very special client?
A princess, in fact!

That princess was Diana, Princess of Wales. Just as a new year marks a new beginning, meeting Princess Diana symbolized a wonderful new beginning in Jimmy's career.

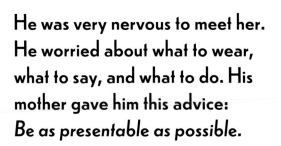

He was very nervous to meet her. He worried about what to wear, what to say, and what to do. His mother gave him this advice: *Be as presentable as possible.*

Following Chinese New Year tradition, Jimmy wore a brand-new outfit from head to toe. He spent every cent he could spare on a new suit. He even bought new underpants and socks!

Jimmy went on to make Diana
many pairs of custom shoes.

Strappy sling-backs. Flat V-shaped pumps. Towering four-inch stilettos. Shoes made from fine grosgrain, shimmering satin, and lustrous silk. Every pair was designed to match one of Diana's dresses.

Whenever Diana wore Jimmy's shoes to an event, the shoes were in the news the next day. And everyone wanted a pair of Choos!

Over seven years and countless visits to
Kensington Palace, Jimmy and Diana became
friends, and Jimmy's career blossomed.

With Diana's royal stamp of approval, clients flocked to Jimmy's workshop. Jimmy's shoes continued to be a celebrity favorite.

Demand was so high, Jimmy decided to expand his business to produce ready-to-wear shoes.

Today, the Jimmy Choo brand is world-famous.
Jimmy still makes shoes for select clients.
But he spends most of his time giving talks around
the world and mentoring young designers.

He will never forget how a poor boy from Penang
became shoemaker to a princess.

AUTHOR'S NOTE

Jimmy Choo was born Choo Yeang Keat in Penang, Malaysia. In Mandarin Chinese, his family name is 周 (Zhōu), which is anglicized to Chow. However, Chow was misspelled as Choo on his birth certificate. If not for this error, the iconic brand would be "Jimmy Chow"!

Growing up in 1950s Penang, Jimmy did normal everyday things like swim in the ocean, hike in the hills, and bike around the island. Jimmy also spent many hours in his father's shoemaking workshop after school.

At twelve, Jimmy left school—Malaysia only required six years of compulsory primary education then—and became a full-time apprentice in his father's workshop.

Jimmy's father was not just a cobbler—he was a talented shoe designer who was one of the best-known shoemakers in Penang. He instilled in young Jimmy a good work ethic and the belief that making shoes is an art form. This experience cultivated young Jimmy's passion for the art of designing and making shoes.

When Penang lost its status as a duty-free port in 1969, fewer visitors came to the island. Fewer visitors meant fewer people were buying merchandise. Businesses like shoemaking suffered. Jimmy's father told him that a good shoemaker could travel the world and make a living. So Jimmy decided to move to London to find a job in shoe designing and making. Eventually, he enrolled at Cordwainers Technical College, now part of the London College of Fashion.

When Jimmy first got to London, he hardly spoke English and had difficulty adapting to his new home. His father paid for his first year of tuition at Cordwainers, but Jimmy worked in a restaurant and a shoe factory to pay for the remaining two years and living expenses. Jimmy persevered and graduated with honors. But his hardships didn't end there.

Jimmy wanted to make luxury couture shoes that were painstakingly made by hand. First, he had to find customers. He made two pairs of shoes a day and sold them at the London Liverpool Street Market. Hoping for good luck, Jimmy sold his first designs under the brand Lucky Shoes. Unfortunately, few people at the flea market wanted to buy his elegant, handmade shoes. He soon realized he had to change tactics. Even though he had always been self-conscious about his faltering English, Jimmy made an

effort to promote himself and build relationships with magazine editors and fashion designers.

In 1988, Jimmy's shoes were featured in a runway show during London Fashion Week. They caught the attention of Vogue, and following the show, Jimmy's shoes were splashed across an eight-page spread in the magazine. The publicity from the Vogue coverage boosted his sales tremendously.

Then, the Princess of Wales discovered Jimmy's shoes through fashion designer Tomasz Starzewski and asked for an introduction. As soon as Jimmy started designing shoes for Diana, his business really took off!

It wasn't long before Jimmy realized there were only so many shoes he and his small team could make by hand. In 1996, Jimmy partnered with former Vogue editor Tamara Mellon to expand his business and produce ready-to-wear shoes under the company Jimmy Choo Ltd. Jimmy sold his half of the company in 2001.

Today, Jimmy continues to make shoes for select clients. He also travels the world speaking at universities and charity events and mentors young Asian designers. Jimmy is a global ambassador of the Alumni Awards for the British Council and an ambassador for the Diana Award, a charity that supports social programs to help young people.

In 2002, Jimmy was conferred the title Order of the British Empire (OBE) in recognition of his services to the shoe and fashion industry in the UK. For his contributions to Malaysia, Jimmy also received the titles Dato and Datuk, both of which are equivalent to a knighthood.

SOURCES

BOOKS

Crowe, Lauren Goldstein. *The Towering World of Jimmy Choo*. New York: Bloomsbury USA, 2009.

Hurst, Brandon. *Jimmy Choo*. Artnik (digital/Kindle edition), 2011.

Sapet, Kerrily. *Jimmy Choo (Profiles in Fashion)*. Greensboro, NC: Morgan Reynolds, 2010.

MAGAZINES

Nash, Emily. "Jimmy Choo on Fun Times with His Sole Mate Diana." *Hello Magazine*, Issue 1476, April 10, 2017.

ONLINE NEWS

"Jimmy Choo: How a Boy from Penang, Malaysia, Became the Shoemaker of Choice for British Royalty, Including Princess Diana." *South China Morning Post*. See www.scmp.com/news/hong-kong/community/article/2153979/jimmy-choo-how-boy-penang-malaysia-became-shoemaker-choice.

"Jimmy Choo Staying True to His Roots." *Independent*. See www.independent.co.uk/life-style/fashion/jimmy-choo-staying-true-to-his-roots-2247873.html.

"Luxury Lineage: A Brief History of Jimmy Choo." *Forbes Lifestyle*. See www.forbes.com/sites/msolomon/2017/08/15/luxury-lineage-a-brief-history-of-jimmy-choo/#24a5b1aa3a2e.

The Reserve: Shoes by Jimmy Choo. See thereserve-asia.com/shoes-by-jimmy-choo.